King of Shadows

Contents

OXFORD
UNIVERSITY PRESS

Great Clarendon Street, Oxford OX2 6DP

Oxford University Press is a department of the University of Oxford. It furthers the University's objective of excellence in research, scholarship, and education by publishing worldwide in

Oxford New York

Auckland Cape Town Dar es Salaam Hong Kong Karachi Kuala Lumpur Madrid Melbourne Mexico City Nairobi New Delhi Shanghai Taipei Toronto

With offices in

Argentina Austria Brazil Chile Czech Republic France Greece Gautamala Hungary Italy Japan South Korea Poland Portugal Singapore Switzerland Thailand Turkey Ukraine Vietnam

Oxford is a registered trade mark of Oxford University Press in the UK and in certain other countries

Text © Gareth Calway 2009

The moral rights of the author have been asserted

Database right Oxford University Press (maker)

First published 2009

All rights reserved. No part of this publication may be reproduced, stored in a retrieval system, or transmitted in any form or by any means, without the prior permission in writing of Oxford University Press, or as expressly permitted by law, or under terms agreed with the appropriate reprographics rights organization. Enquiries concerning reproduction outside the scope of the above should be sent to the Rights Department, Oxford University Press, at the address above.

You must not circulate this book in any other binding or cover and you must impose this same condition on any acquirer.

British Library Cataloguing in Publication Data

Data available

ISBN 978 019 832894 0

10 9 8 7 6 5 4 3 2 1

Printed in China by Printplus

Acknowledgements

The Publisher would like to thank the following for permission to reproduce photographs:

P3 & p14 Susan Cooper; p4 Pawel Libera/Shakespeare's Globe Theatre; p4 Mary Evans Picture Library/Alamy; p5 Mary Evans Picture Library; p6 & p14 Robert Harding Picture Library Ltd/ Alamy; p10 Science Photo Library; p12 Adina TovyArt Directors & Trip Photo Library; p13 Alastair Muir/Rex Features; p14 Guido Alberto Rossi/Photolibrary

Illustrations are by Steve Evans Design and Illustration

Front cover photograph Alamy

We are grateful for permission to reprint the following copyright material in this guide:

Susan Cooper: extracts from *King of Shadows* (Bodley Head, 1999) and book cover blurb reprinted by permission of the Random House Group Ltd; letter and notes reprinted by permission of the author.

We have tried to trace and contact all copyright holders before publication. If notified, the publisher will be pleased to rectify any errors or omissions at the earliest opportunity.

Answers to the crossword on page 5

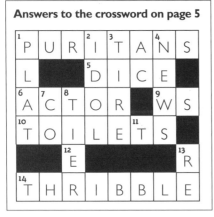

Answers to the quiz on page 6

1 Stratford-upon-Avon
2 Rumour says he died from a fever, which may have been typhus, caught in a pub.
3 He didn't go to university. After Stratford Grammar School, he had to earn a living in London.
4 He wasn't particularly rich and needed a powerful patron like the Earl of Southampton. He worked hard until 1611 and then retired to Stratford.
5 Some called him an 'upstart crow', but Queen Elizabeth I thought highly of him and he was loved by his audiences.
6 He married Anne Hathaway and they had a daughter and boy-girl twins. Hamnet died as a boy.

King of Shadows

A Letter from Susan Cooper

Dear Readers,

I've always been stage-struck. When I was three years old, my parents took me to the local pantomime and apparently I sat through it entranced and burst into tears when the curtain came down. The rest of the audience left peacefully, but I had to be carried out, screaming. I just didn't want the play to end.

Then when I was 12, I was lucky enough to see my first live Shakespeare play. George Devine's original Young Vic Company came to our school with *The Merchant of Venice* and I was entranced all over again. Suddenly the name Shakespeare no longer meant difficult words on a page but an astonishing, funny, scary, sexy *happening*. From that moment on, I was obsessed not only with theatre but with Shakespeare – not as 'the Bard' but as a working actor-playwright.

For that's what he was – this amazing man, the greatest writer we've ever produced – he was a professional actor-playwright, trying to get audiences through the door by providing his fellow actors with terrific stories and great parts. He wasn't – as some people would have you believe – the Earl of Oxford hiding behind a pseudonym or a collection of other more learned writers. He was Will Shakespeare, man of the theatre. And the older I grew, watching and reading his plays, the more I wished I could have met him. When I wrote the biggest work of my own life, a five-book sequence called *The Dark Is Rising*, I named my hero after him – Will.

And one day I realized that I could, in fact, meet Will Shakespeare. After all, a writer's imagination can take him or her anywhere. So I put myself inside a modern boy actor about to play Puck at the rebuilt Globe Theatre, who finds himself transported back in time to Shakespeare's Globe. Like me, he falls in love with Shakespeare – and in an extraordinary way manages to save his life, and perhaps his own life too.

So now you'll find out how that happens. I hope you like the book. After you've read it, please, please go to see a Shakespeare play *on the stage*.

Susan Cooper

Rebuilding Shakespeare's Globe

Susan Cooper, the author of *King of Shadows*, seems to have had quite an obsession with Shakespeare and his Globe Theatre.

Groundbreaker Wanamaker

More than 40 years ago, I interviewed Sam Wanamaker, the American actor living in London, who was later the original driving force behind the building of the reproduced Globe. I was a young reporter on 'The Sunday Times' and I never forgot his obsession with Shakespeare's theatre because I shared it myself.

Sam Wanamaker missed Shakespeare's original Globe Theatre so much that he built a new one in the same place! He wanted it to have a thatched roof and a timber frame of green oak, just like Shakespeare's original. Sam spent 25 years collecting private donations for it. Building finally began in 1993 – too late for Sam, who died shortly after the groundbreaking – but not for the audiences who would soon be flocking there to see the plays they loved in the original open-air conditions, just as they had in Shakespeare's day.

Where obsessions lead

- ◎ What do you think Susan Cooper did to pursue her obsession for Shakespeare's theatre? (Read her letter on page 3 for clues.)
- ◎ Shakespeare can be performed on any kind of stage. Why do you think Sam wanted to reproduce the original Globe Theatre?

No bears, no devils, no actors

In 1583, about the time Shakespeare arrived in London, the pamphleteer Phillip Stubbes declared that all stage plays are 'sucked out of the Deuills teates to nourish us in ydolatrie, hethenrie, and sinne'!

Deuills teates the devil is feeding playgoers with evil, like an animal feeding its young
hethenrie not believing in the Christian God
ydolatrie worship of manmade objects
popishness costumed plays felt to resemble Catholic Mass
Puritans Protestants who wanted stricter moral behaviour

A Plague On All Their Houses

Churchmen believe God is showing his wrath on the play-acting profession! We had an earthquake in 1580, a serious brawl outside a theatre in the mid-1580s and the collapse of wooden scaffolding at a bear-baiting show, killing several people. Worse – since 1581 the 'ungodliness' of plays has brought on the plague like a curse from Heaven and gatherings in the playhouse have caused it to spread. Puritans also blame the theatres for sinful men dressing up in women's clothes, popishness, and bringing violence, traffic congestion, and wildness around taverns.

The mischievous Puck

London authorities refused to allow plays in the city. So theatres moved across the Thames to Southwark where they had more freedom. Before the first one – The Theatre – was built at Shoreditch in 1576, plays were put on by travelling actors, whose wooden wagons became makeshift stages. They performed in the courtyards of inns or the houses of noblemen daring enough to risk the political trouble a play could bring. The original Globe Theatre was built in 1599.

Diabolical consequences

◎   Is there anything dangerous – even diabolical – about Nat's theatre experiences in Chapter 1?

◎   Improvise a phone call from a parent complaining to Arby about his theatre classes.

How much can you answer so far?

Try 1 across, and 1 and 2 down for starters.

Across
1   They hated the theatres (8)
5   'I throw the ____, Tom, I throw the ____.' (4)
6   Nat's dream job (5)
9   Nat's hero (initials) (2)
10   Original Globe was unlikely to have these! (7)
12   Silent letter in Shakespeare's name – and he never used it (1)
14   What you do when you forget your lines (8)

Down
1   The order of scenes (Elizabethan spelling). Add form and you have a stage! (4)
2   What Shakespeare is to both Nat and Susan Cooper (4)
3   Costume (4)
4   'How now, what ___?' How new information was often introduced on stage (4)
7   Short for 'company' (2)
8   Row of seats in a theatre (4)
13   Two letters in both Romeo and Oberon – but only once! (2)

What a Character!

Quick Quiz

Think you know Shakespeare?

1 Where was he born?
2 How did he die?
3 What university did he go to?
4 Was he rich or poor?
5 Was he as revered then as he is now?
6 Did he marry and have children?

Answers are on page 2.

Shakespeare in the hot seat

Use the Quick Quiz as a starting point for putting Shakespeare in the hot seat. What sort of answers would he give to questions like 'How do you feel about not being a university man like Kit Marlowe?'

Dost miss thy parents?

My dad missed my mum. I tried to be enough for him, but I wasn't.

Do not say thou wast not enough for thy father. Some things are beyond our command.

Nat breaks down and describes his father's suicide to Shakespeare. Read the passage on pages 70–72.

Discussion points

- Nat has a vivid image of 'a pool of red blood, spreading'. Where have you read that before? Why does it upset him so much?
- How does Shakespeare act towards Nat here? What evidence is there?
- What private grief does Shakespeare share with Nat?
- What is Nat and Shakespeare's relationship like?

Understanding love

Love is not love
Which alters when it alteration finds,
Or bends with the remover to remove.
Oh no! It is an ever fixed mark.

Shakespeare gives Nat a copy of a sonnet (on pages 101–102) to help him understand his father's suicide. Discuss what it means and how it's relevant to Nat's situation.

King of Shadows

Where there's a Will, there's a Nat, Rich, Kit ...

The Globe

Nathan Field

THEATRE PASS

Dates: 1587–1619
Profession: actor, and playwright of two comedies
Education: St Paul's School
Work experience:
- Children of the Chapel acting company
- Children of the Queen's Revels acting company from 1600
- King's Men from 1609 (may have taken Shakespeare's place as actor/shareholder in 1616)

Famous for: being one of the leading actors listed in Shakespeare's First Folio

The Globe

Richard Burbage

THEATRE PASS

Dates: 1568–1619
Profession: actor, theatre owner and artist
Work experience:
- inherited Blackfriars Theatre and The Theatre from his father
- moved The Theatre over the Thames and renamed it the Globe
- Lord Chamberlain's Men (the King's Men from 1603)

Famous for: performing tragic parts by Shakespeare, Jonson and others

Staging a role call

- ◎ Look at the theatre passes (above) of people Shakespeare knew. Research and compile similar details for other people he knew or key people in his world, like Kit Marlowe, the Earls of Essex or Southampton and Queen Elizabeth I.
- ◎ In a group, each take the role of one person. Pose for a photograph, sitting close or far away from Shakespeare, who sits in the middle, according to how important your character was to him.
- ◎ Display your photograph and biography details.

Discussion points

- ◎ How important are these characters to Nat in the novel?
- ◎ What part do these characters play in *King of Shadows*?
- ◎ How does Susan Cooper make them seem real?

Arby bargy

- ◎ Reread page 60. Did Nat deserve the whack?
- ◎ In pairs, improvise what would happen if Burbage summoned Nat to explain the trap door incident.
- ◎ Compare Burbage and Arby, including their attitude to children. (Look at pages 47–48, 60, 109–110, 175–177.)
- ◎ Who would you rather have as a drama teacher? Explain why.

King of Shadows

Time-slip to London 1599

Play the game like 'Snakes and Ladders', with two to six players. Use one die and a small coin as your counter.

- Before each go, say 'I throw the dice, Tom… I throw the dice.' If you forget, you lose your go.
- If you throw 6 and can find a relevant quotation from the novel for your new square within 20 seconds, throw again immediately.
- When you hit the 'Dice Fall' wall, throw again. 1–3 takes you to 1599, and 4 and 5 are void in the 1599 side of the game. 4–6 takes you to square 12 in the twenty-first century.
- If you are following forward instructions from square 9 or square 11, go straight through the 'Dice Fall' wall into 1599. You cannot enter the twenty-first century.
- The final throw must be exact. Overthrows take you back down the board.

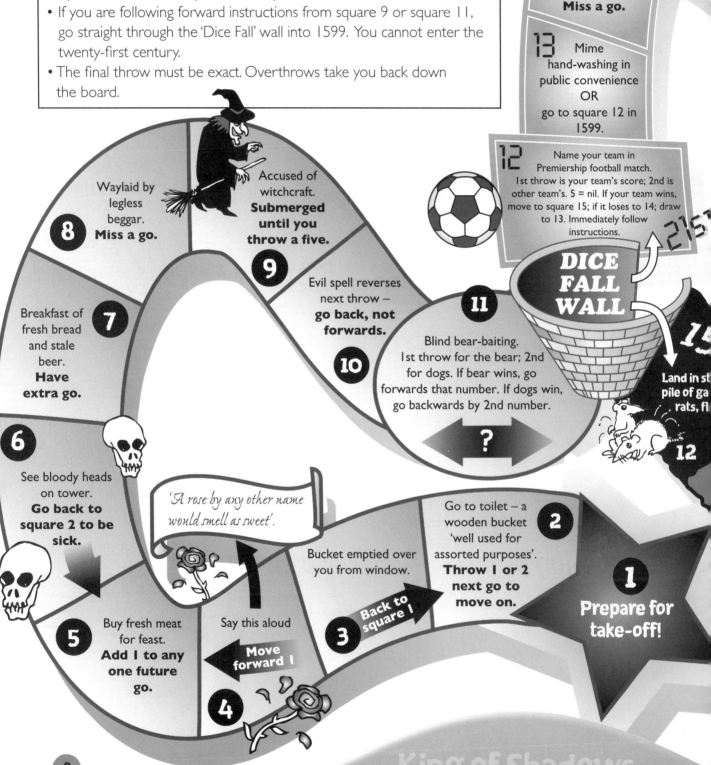

15 Break plastic cutlery.

Go back 1 square

14 Mime eating chicken and chips. **Miss a go.**

13 Mime hand-washing in public convenience OR go to square 12 in 1599.

12 Name your team in Premiership football match. 1st throw is your team's score; 2nd is other team's. 5 = nil. If your team wins, move to square 15; if it loses to 14; draw to 13. Immediately follow instructions.

DICE FALL WALL

21ST

15 Land in st pile of ga rats, fl

12

8 Waylaid by legless beggar. **Miss a go.**

9 Accused of witchcraft. **Submerged until you throw a five.**

7 Breakfast of fresh bread and stale beer. **Have extra go.**

10 Evil spell reverses next throw – **go back, not forwards.**

11 Blind bear-baiting. 1st throw for the bear; 2nd for dogs. If bear wins, go forwards that number. If dogs win, go backwards by 2nd number.

?

6 See bloody heads on tower. **Go back to square 2 to be sick.**

'A rose by any other name would smell as sweet'.

2 Go to toilet – a wooden bucket 'well used for assorted purposes'. **Throw 1 or 2 next go to move on.**

Bucket emptied over you from window.

Back to square 1

3

1 Prepare for take-off!

5 Buy fresh meat for feast. **Add 1 to any one future go.**

Say this aloud

Move forward 1

4

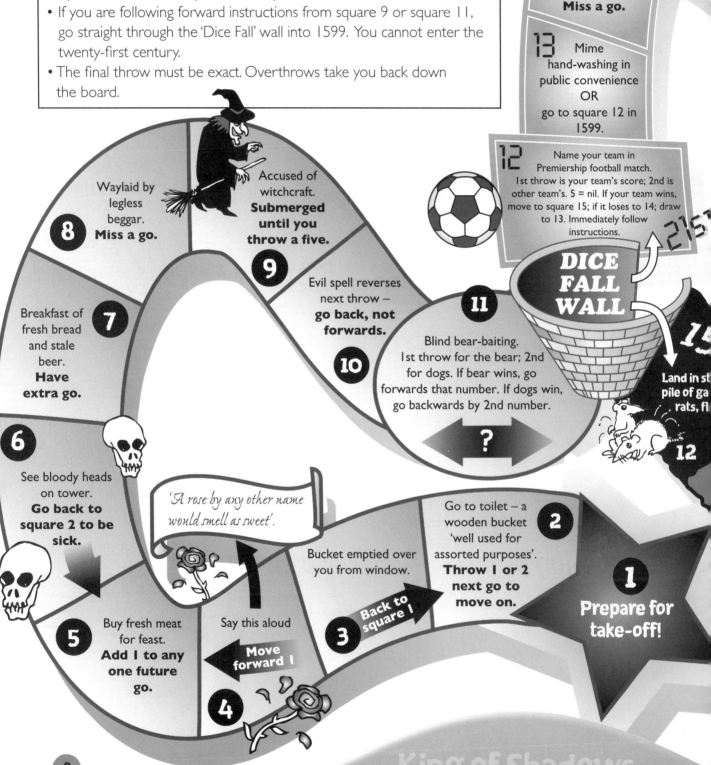

King of Shadows

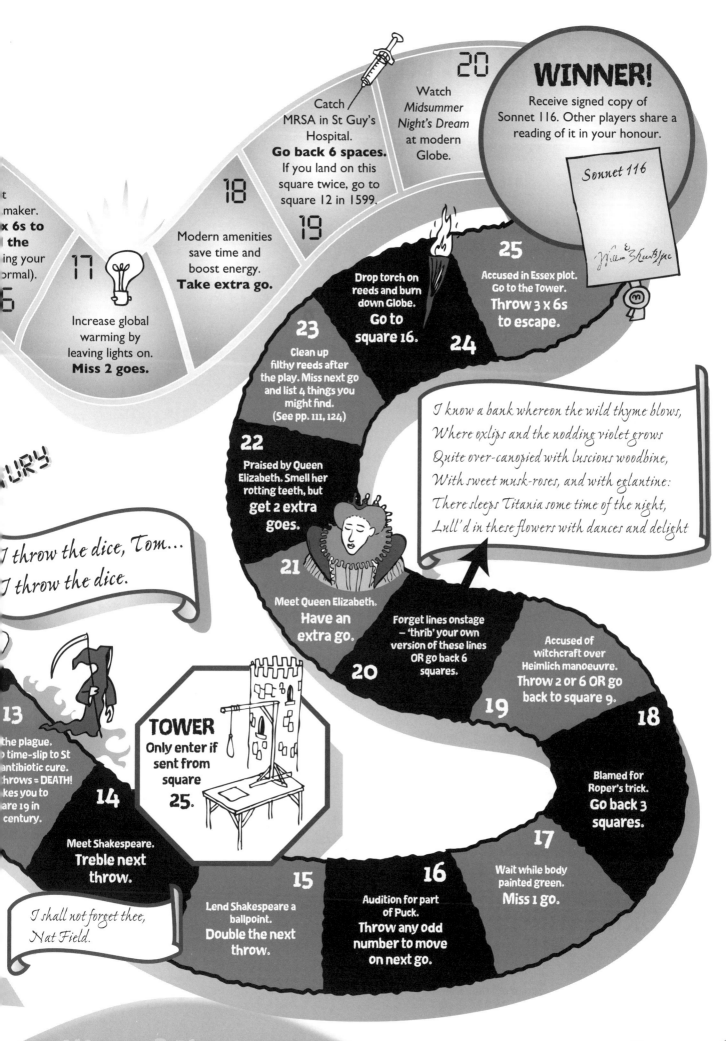

WINNER!
Receive signed copy of Sonnet 116. Other players share a reading of it in your honour.

Sonnet 116

20
Watch *Midsummer Night's Dream* at modern Globe.

Catch MRSA in St Guy's Hospital. **Go back 6 spaces.** If you land on this square twice, go to square 12 in 1599.

18

19

17
Increase global warming by leaving lights on. **Miss 2 goes.**

Modern amenities save time and boost energy. **Take extra go.**

maker. x 6s to the ing your ormal).

25
Accused in Essex plot. Go to the Tower. **Throw 3 x 6s to escape.**

Drop torch on reeds and burn down Globe. **Go to square 16.**

24

23
Clean up filthy reeds after the play. Miss next go and list 4 things you might find. (See pp. 111, 124)

22
Praised by Queen Elizabeth. Smell her rotting teeth, but **get 2 extra goes.**

21
Meet Queen Elizabeth. **Have an extra go.**

I know a bank whereon the wild thyme blows,
Where oxlips and the nodding violet grows
Quite over-canopied with luscious woodbine,
With sweet musk-roses, and with eglantine:
There sleeps Titania some time of the night,
Lull'd in these flowers with dances and delight

I throw the dice, Tom...
I throw the dice.

URY

20
Forget lines onstage – 'thrib' your own version of these lines OR go back 6 squares.

19

Accused of witchcraft over Heimlich manoeuvre. **Throw 2 or 6 OR go back to square 9.**

18

TOWER Only enter if sent from square **25.**

13
the plague. time-slip to St antibiotic cure. hrows = DEATH! kes you to are 19 in century.

14
Meet Shakespeare. **Treble next throw.**

Blamed for Roper's trick. **Go back 3 squares.**

17
Wait while body painted green. **Miss 1 go.**

16
Audition for part of Puck. **Throw any odd number to move on next go.**

15
Lend Shakespeare a ballpoint. **Double the next throw.**

I shall not forget thee, Nat Field.

Saving Shakespeare

A plague upon your house

In *King of Shadows*, Shakespeare is 'saved' from the plague, one of many dangers at that time. The plague wiped out over a quarter of London's population in the epidemic of 1563 – and again in 1603. Survival rates were 50:50.

> Death... hath pitched his tents, (being nothing but a heape of winding sheets tacked together) in the sinfully-polluted Suburbes; the Plague is Muster-maister and Marshall of the field; Burning Feavers, Boyles, Blaines, and Carbuncles, the Leaders...; the maine Army consisting of... dumpish Mourners, merry Sextons, hungry Coffin-sellers, scrubbing Bearers, and nastie Grave-makers; ... Feare and Trembling (the two catch-polles of Death) arrest every one.
>
> Thomas Dekker, pamphleteer, 1603

A plague on you!

Check out the symptoms Nat suffers from on pages 40 and 75. How do they compare with Dekker's account (above)?

Shakespeare faced ruin in 1592–93 when the theatres were closed because of the plague. His later plays, like *Romeo and Juliet* and *King Lear*, often refer to it.

Although Shakespeare escaped the plague, other diseases were also a risk.

> thou art a boil,
> A plague-sore, an embossed carbuncle,
> In my corrupted blood.

King Lear 2:4:242

Queen Elizabeth lost her hair and complexion to **smallpox** in 1562 and wore thick lead/egg white makeup and wigs ever after.

Typhus was carried by lice attracted to the sores on Londoners' itchy, unwashed skin.

Marshy Southwark was a high-risk area for the **ague** (malaria) – even King James caught it.

Sailors brought the **pox** from the Americas – it rotted the body and drove people mad.

Dicing with death

◉ Find any examples in the novel where Shakespeare or Nat is in danger from the plague, any other disease, or accusation as a witch.

◉ In the novel, what are Shakespeare's and Nat's attitudes to cutpurses, danger, and witchcraft?

Playing it dangerously

Shakespeare 'threw the dice' for high stakes at a very tense period of Elizabeth's reign. With the Earl of Southampton as his patron and writing speeches in praise of Essex, he was risking arrest – and maybe much worse.

> The greatest and most grievous punishment used in England for such as offend against the State is drawing from the prison to the place of execution upon an hurdle or sled, where they are hanged till they be half dead, and then taken down, and quartered alive; after that, their members and bowels are cut from their bodies, and thrown into a fire, provided near hand and within their own sight, even for the same purpose.
>
> William Harrison, Elizabethan chronicler

The theatres in Southwark were on the 'wrong side of the river' and full of characters. Shakespeare saw it all. Meet his comic thief, Autolycus from 'The Winter's Tale', who steals washing and other 'trifles' to sell, all the while checking out the 'festival purses'!

> 'My traffic is sheets... I am a snapper up of unconsidered trifles... Ha, ha! What a fool Honesty is... I have sold all my trumpery; not a counterfeit stone, not a ribbon, glass, pomander, brooch, table-book... to keep my pack from fasting... by which means I saw whose purse was best in picture; and what I saw I remembered... twas nothing to geld a codpiece of a purse; I would have fil'd off that hung in chains... So that in this time of lethargy I pick'd and cut most of their festival purses...'

Time travel tour

Imagine Nat is introducing Shakespeare to the twenty-first century. How would Shakespeare react to the things below (or any of the things on page 65)? In pairs, play the parts of Nat and Shakespeare.

Living in 1599 was like being on a permanent camping trip in a third world country.

texting   music   sport

TV soaps   PCs   The X Factor

The Bankside Globe Trotters

The travelling acting companies attracted disorder. Audiences ate, drank, and created problems during performances. Pickpockets, beggars, prostitutes, and other 'undesirables' thrived in the large crowds – as did the plague.

So, from the late 1500s, acting companies sought the respectability of noble or royal sponsorship. The patrons lent their names, though not their money. The Lord Chamberlain (Henry Carey and then his son George) sponsored Shakespeare's company, the Lord Chamberlain's Men. Later King James adopted it and it became The King's Men. Such companies performed in playhouses and private theatres.

The Actors

Elizabethan acting companies had roughly ten shareholders, several salaried actors, and apprentices to the senior actors. Women were not allowed – playhouses were too rough! Instead, boy apprentices acted the female characters. Each actor tended to play the same type of role – a fool, hero, or clown – but needed to be able to play multiple parts in one play, tumble, dance, and fence – as well as remember his lines.

Staging in Shakespeare's theatres

In a film, if an actor gestures towards 'yonder forest' you expect to see a forest scene, but audiences in 1599 needed to use their imaginations – there wasn't any scenery. Up to 3000 people paid to be shut into a wooden-framed theatre, expecting to spend two or three hours enjoying a play that conjured up many such illusions. However, churchmen said that any act of deception like that was the Devil's work, so players could be accused of being the Devil's agents.

Around the Globe

◎ Imagine you are Harry taking Nat on a tour round the Globe Theatre. As you go, explain how a play was staged and introduce the characters and what they did.

◎ Sketch a timetable of Nat's typical day at the Globe's theatre school. Include lunch, interruptions like Roper being nasty to him, and how well Nat did in each class.

This distracted globe

In a theatre, you are part of what Hamlet called 'this distracted globe' – a place where your mind is distracted from the real things outside. Shakespeare often experimented with the idea of a play being an illusion like this, or even a dream.

An American in London

Susan Cooper's research notes explore Nat's journey away from 'reality' in the modern world.

Tube to Mansion House station. Turn right, go down Garlick Hill and left on to Skinners Lane. Turn right, and there's Southwark Bridge, which wasn't there in Shakespeare's time.

Maybe when Nat comes back to the 20th century you bring him from the theatre to the Tube station, and he remembers Garlick Hill from 300 years before – only now there are people walking along talking on mobile phones, and a smell of pizza...

A Midsummer Night's Dream

Oberon and Titania, king and queen of fairyland, have quarrelled!

Oberon applies the juice of a magic flower to Titania's eyes. She wakes and falls in love with Bottom – despite his Ass's head! Puck puts magic juice into Lysander's eyes instead of Demetrius's, so the wrong man falls in love with Helena.

A wonderful comic confusion – for us, if not for the lovers!

Discussion points

◎ How does Susan Cooper get Nat back to his own time in the final version?
◎ Find the two time-slips in the novel, there and back. What do they have in common? What is new and/or special about the second one?
◎ What does Nat's experience have in common with the play that he's in?

Living history

How has Susan Cooper brought her research alive? Choose three of the following topics and find examples of them in the novel. What language is particularly effective in making the characters and events seem real – pleasant or unpleasant?

Patrons

Queen Elizabeth

Plague

Witchcraft

Shakespeare

Actors

Burbage

Executions

Cutpurses

Susan Cooper's Time Machine

'Go and see a Shakespeare play on the stage.'

In her letter on page 3, Susan Cooper emphasizes the transporting magic of theatre and of a writer's imagination. She says she was 'stage struck', 'entranced', and that 'I could meet Will Shakespeare… a writer's imagination can take them anywhere.'

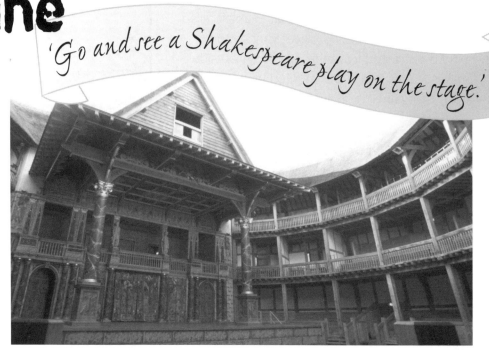

A tardis to Shakespeare's England

How dost thou write a novel?

When I'm writing a book, I write the actual text on the right-hand page, and on the left-hand page I talk to myself… it's those left-hand pages that show me where the book will go and what I must find out before I go on writing.

Here are some of Susan Cooper's notes from when she was beginning to write 'the Shakespeare book'.

• I think where this chapter [1] is going is an explosion between RB and Nat revealing that Nat feels responsible for his father's death. Did the father kill himself? Does RB not know that?

• Chapter 2 is the modern Globe, and after that the family Nat is staying with. (They live somewhere that must be an equivalent of the place where Nathan and Dick live in the 16th c.)
… Nat's head is singing; he feels unreal. And it's in that unreality, while he is half asleep, half in fever, that the time-slip takes place.

Interview Susan Cooper

Imagine you can interview her. What would you ask her about the novel? Here are some ideas:

◎ What was the real reason for Nat's time-slip? Was it caused by the intensity of his grief and anger, a fever dream, the magic of theatre — or simply your imagination?

◎ What did Nat get from Shakespeare that cured his grief?

◎ What do you think writers' imaginations give to people that can cure them of real-life problems?

King of Shadows

Guess the time-slip, or world-slip, stories from these clues.
- A tunnel in Carlisle leads to a 17th-century world of lawless borderers.
- A warehouse in Cardiff crosses a time rift.
- An old hallway at midnight leads into a garden.
- A Greek forest leads lost lovers and actors into fairyland.
- A hollow hill introduces past and future kings.
- A wardrobe gives way to woods and a lamppost.
- The mind of an unusual boy leads at midwinter to his destiny as an 'Old One'.
- A police box goes where it wants in the universe.

Spending an olde pennie

Susan Cooper talks to herself about Nat's time-slip.

Time to escape

◎ Think of your own time-slip device. Your time-traveller doesn't need to be mad – with grief or fever, or about the stage – but it may help!

◎ Design a book cover and write a blurb for your story. Think carefully about the colours, font and pictures you will use to suggest the time-slip.

In the past, Harry is peering at Nat. How are you? Is your fever less? He's keeping a cautious distance.

Who are you?

Are you still unwell? I'm Harry, of course, Harry your fellow. Are you out of your wits, Nat?

I feel better. But – he looks around him. He's in the 16th century. He's aghast.

Harry is babbling nervously. Do you remember last night?

No, not really.

They brought you home in a cart, your fever was so high. I was afraid you had the plague. But you haven't, have you? You'd be dead by now, or on the way.

I... do feel better.

Get up, then –

Everything is unfamiliar. Where does he pee? What does he wear? Where and what do they eat? It's 1599, what is happening in England? (So I went

Pathways... to Another Good Read

Other books by Susan Cooper

Victory
ISBN: 019 8326786
Sam is a farm boy, press ganged to serve aboard *HMS Victory*, Lord Nelson's ship. Molly is a modern English girl forced to live in America. This extraordinary time-shifting adventure tells their interwoven stories – two lives linked by one fragment of history.

The Dark is Rising series
ISBN: 037 0329422
Eleven-year-old Will learns that he is the last of the Old Ones and must lead the forces of the Light in an ancient struggle with the Dark. The fabulous adventures that follow have an Arthurian atmosphere and are full of dark menace and thrills.

Other time-slip books

The Sterkarm Handshake by Susan Price
ISBN: 006 0293926
A time tube takes Andrea back to the Scottish borders in the 1500s. The Sterkarm warriors are welcoming at first – but things get complicated when Andrea falls in love with Per Sterkarm, who is then fatally injured. Beware of the Sterkarms' handshake!

Cue For Treason by Geoffrey Trease
ISBN: 014 030231X
Fleeing injustice in Elizabethan England, Peter meets Kit, another runaway. As apprentices to William Shakespeare, Kit's unusual circumstances bring extra danger to their difficult lives. This book has mystery, drama, twists, and thrilling action – and a Shakespeare to compare with Susan Cooper's.

In the Nick of Time by Robert Swindells
ISBN: 019 8328957
When Charlie falls off a stepping stone in the woods, her whole world changes. She finds herself in 1952 – and in a weird outdoor school where the classrooms don't even have walls. Can new friend Jack help her back through the nick in time – or will she be trapped in the past?

Tom's Midnight Garden by Philippa Pearce
ISBN: 019 2792423
Tom is sent to his aunt's house for the summer. When the grandfather clock strikes thirteen instead of one, the adventures start. Outside, he finds a beautiful garden. There are children in the garden – or ghosts… Or is he the ghost?

Timesnatch by Robert Swindells
ISBN: 055 2555924
Kitty and Fraser discover that extinct animals are not gone forever when they travel back to the past in their mother's time machine. The machine is amazing, but it leads them into terrifyingly sinister situations of mind-boggling proportions.

Stratford Boys by Jan Mark
ISBN: 034 0860987
Teenage Will Shakespeare ropes in his friends and neighbours – the Stratford Boys – to help him entertain the locals. Find out how he manages to write and stage his first play against all the odds. It's met by thunderous applause, so it could be the start of an amazing career!

King of Shadows